THE WASTE LAND

AND

OTHER POEMS

JOHN BEER

‹CANARIUM BOOKS
ANN ARBOR, BERKELEY, IOWA CITY

SPONSORED BY
THE UNIVERSITY OF MICHIGAN
CREATIVE WRITING PROGRAM

THE WASTE LAND

AND

OTHER POEMS

Canarium Books
Ann Arbor, Berkeley, Iowa City
www.canariumbooks.org

The editors gratefully acknowledge the
University of Michigan Creative Writing Program
for editorial assistance and generous support.

Cover: Facsimile of the back cover of the 1923
Hogarth Press edition of T. S. Eliot's *The Waste Land*,
courtesy of the Poetry Collection, University at Buffalo,
the State University of New York.

Design: Gou Dao Niao

First edition
Second printing

Printed in the United States of America

ISBN-13: 978-0-9822376-4-9

for my parents
and
in memory of
Robert Lax
(1915-2000)

I obeyed the instructions as best I could, though the powerful gusts made it difficult to maintain a suitably genial expression on my face.

Kazuo Ishiguro

CONTENTS

Drip   drip   drip   drip   drip   drip   drop
Drip   drop   drop   drip   drop   drop   drop
Drop   drip   drip   drip   drip   drop   drip
Drip   drip   drip   drop   drip   drop   drip

Drop   drop   drop   drip   drop   drip   drop
Drop   drop   drop   drip   drop   drop   drip
Drip   drip   drop   drop   drip   drip   drop
Drop   drop   drip   drip   drop   drop   drop

Drop   drip   drop   drop   drop   drip   drop
Drip   drop   drop   drip   drop   drop   drip
Drop   drop   drip   drip   drop   drop   drip
Drop   drip   drop   drop   drip   drip   drop

Drip   drop   drip   drop   drip   drip   drip
Drop   drip   drop   drip   drip   drip   drop
Drop   drip   drop   drip   drop   drip   drop
Drop   drip   drip   drop   drop   drip   drip

Drip   drop   drip   drop   drop   drop   drop
Drip   drop   drip   drop   drop   drip   drip
Drop   drop   drop   drop   drop   drip   drip
Drip   drip   drop   drip   drop   drip   drop

Drop   drop   drop   drip   drip   drop   drip
Drip   drip   drip   drop   drip   drip   drip
Drop   drop   drip   drip   drop   drip   drip
Drop   drop   drop   drip   drip   drop   drop

Drip	drip	drip	drip	drip	drip	drop
Drip	drop	drop	drip	drop	drop	drop
Drop	drip	drip	drip	drip	drop	drip
Drip	drip	drip	drop	drip	drop	drip

Drop	drop	drop	drip	drop	drip	drop
Drop	drop	drop	drip	drop	drop	drip
Drip	drip	drop	drop	drip	drip	drop
Drop	drop	drip	drip	drop	drop	drop

Drop	drip	drop	drop	drop	drip	drop
Drip	drop	drop	drip	drop	drop	drip
Drop	drop	drip	drip	drop	drop	drip
Drop	drip	drop	drop	drip	drip	drop

Drip	drop	drip	drop	drip	drip	drip
Drop	drip	drop	drip	drip	drip	drop
Drop	drip	drop	drip	drop	drip	drop
Drop	drip	drip	drop	drop	drip	drip

Drip	drop	drip	drop	drop	drop	drop
Drip	drop	drip	drop	drop	drip	drip
Drop	drop	drop	drop	drop	drip	drip
Drip	drip	drop	drip	drop	drip	drop

Drop	drop	drop	drip	drip	drop	drip
Drip	drip	drip	drop	drip	drip	drip
Drop	drop	drip	drip	drop	drip	drip
Drop	drop	drop	drip	drip	drop	drop

Drip	drip	drip	drip	drip	drip	drop
Drip	drop	drop	drip	drop	drop	drop
Drop	drip	drip	drip	drip	drop	drip
Drip	drip	drip	drop	drip	drop	drip
Drop	drop	drop	drip	drop	drip	drop
Drop	drop	drop	drip	drop	drop	drip
Drip	drip	drop	drop	drip	drip	drop
Drop	drop	drip	drip	drop	drop	drop
Drop	drip	drop	drop	drop	drip	drop
Drip	drop	drop	drip	drop	drop	drip
Drop	drop	drip	drip	drop	drop	drip
Drop	drip	drop	drop	drip	drip	drop
Drip	drop	drip	drop	drip	drip	drip
Drop	drip	drop	drip	drip	drip	drop
Drop	drip	drop	drip	drop	drip	drop
Drop	drip	drip	drop	drop	drip	drip

THE WASTE LAND

'*Aber die Thronen, wo? Die Tempel, und wo die Gefäße,*
Wo mit Nectar gefüllt, Göttern zu Lust der Gesang?'

'*Someone's got it in for me*'

for Jack Spicer
the fabber craftsman

I. THE FUNERAL MARCH (CHICAGO AND ORLEANS)

Once more in the city I cannot name,
the boat city, the city of light,
the city that endures its fall,
the city of pleasures and vicissitudes,
the skier's city, Fun City, the city under the sky,
city of crime and vegetables, Pornograph City,
the city governed by the Lost and Found Department,
cabinet city, city of the bends, the opium city,
Swing City, Archetype City, city of dust,
city that eludes the seven ages, muskrat city,
the island city of daughters and wives,
Sin City, city of sincerity, the cavernous city,
the city of conventions, hatmaker city,
Alphabet City, city of the last and first,
the city called Marrakesh (I know it is not Marrakesh),
industrial city, the city of airplane booze,
center city, the city without shoulders, the city that forgot,
the trampoline city, Abacus City, the city of tears,
the real city (or the city of the desert),
the unreal city (or the city of good will),
the city of rust, of showers, of late blooming aster,
Hygiene City, the city of logistics—
once more in the city called Halloween
(I know it is not Halloween), I gathered
the five true ingredients of gunpowder
and arranged to meet my younger brother Stetson
next noon at the Heartland Cafe.

Why do you walk with your face turned from me?
All you do is complain and complain.
What is this thing called love? It is nothing
reliable, not like this silk cravat
on which tiny turtles hover
suspended against an amber background.
The knot needs to be loosened. Night has come.
I walk in the garden amid the late-blooming roses
and guard my glass from the moon.
This morning the police came for me.
They brought a letter covered with signs
I could not decipher. They demanded
I register my address properly,
because they are sorely tested by the time's demands
and cannot function as my delivery service.
I met their angry gazes with a sigh, and I proclaimed:
"April is the coolest month, which brings
happy policemen the pleasant dreams of spring."
They still refused to answer my questions.
I know my life is in terrible danger.
What is this thing called love?

II. DON'T LOOK BACK

A degree or two to the right
of an imagined meridian
marking time's monotonous ecliptic
tracing and retracing the animal steps

that bring the man down narrow hallways,
a painting hangs, depicting
an almond tree in blossom, unfurling
white petals against a deepening green,
brown brushstrokes scarring the field,
and in the center of the decentered vista,
a fleck of canvas erupts through the paint,
as when air thrusts itself to fill a vacuum,
or after galactic gyrations the light
of a now-cold star reveals itself to us
and breaks the settled pattern of the sky.
For if the tree implies a quiet place
where pendulums might rest,
the heart decline to beat, a place
of time disclosing the lattice of time,
each node identical, complete within itself,
its infinite simplicity sufficient
to lure the mind out of its droning dream
of traffic, footstools, marzipan, and clouds
back to itself, if the tree must be a sign
of the viewer's hunger to escape from signs
and thereby lose the world, the tiny scar
unmakes the fiction that sustains the tree,
the way a cashier's knowing jibe
at the record you had waited weeks to buy,
recommended to you by a woman you barely know
who mentioned it in passing, then returned
to her diatribe against the host who failed
to invite her boyfriend or her companion's boyfriend—
you had only half been listening until she said,
"It sounds like nothing else, not like the wind

or ocean, not even like the early Pixies,
though it has that effect on you, something like
getting a letter addressed to someone else
that ends up addressed to you, in that
reading it with a proper sense of shame
throws your devotion to formalities
completely out the window. I think they're from New York,"
and meant to ask her how the band was spelled,
but the moment had passed, your cigarettes were out,
and the birdless night grew colder. You returned
to people you felt more familiar with,
the oddly Teutonic name in the back of your mind,
and only later came across it in the discount bin
of the Princeton Record Exchange, whose clerks
everyone knows are assholes, so the sneer
on the Tom Verlaine guy's lips was no surprise,
though it gripped you with a sense as far from panic
as it resembled exile. No song can bear
the weight we need to place upon it;
nothing returns as we ask it to return.

O O that T. S. Eliot
he's such a shrinking violet
and if you think I sigh a lot
try life with T. S. Eliot

Sam's problem was he would always compare himself
to other people. I told him, Sam, you don't need to be
a hero. But now I can see I was wrong. I wanted him
to be heroic, but not in that guerrilla theater way.
I told him, Sam, it's time to take off the puppet head.

You could give him a little credit, though, for standing up
against corporate hegemony. He always buys his coffee
from locally owned establishments, and he shoplifts
all those books of poetry from Barnes and Noble.
Oh, everyone deserves a little credit. All the angry
little men in angry little rooms can write
their diagnoses, xerox their zines, and dream
that someday they'll become the next Debord.
In the meantime, how am I supposed to live?
None of us is getting any younger. Power clutches
THANK YOU FOR SHOPPING AT BORDERS.
WE WILL BE CLOSING IN FIFTEEN MINUTES.
everyone with a velvet embrace. But isn't
a life deformed by constant struggle a life
as much defined by power's rule as one
in which you carve a space out for yourself?
I want to find my happiness on my own terms.
That's what we all want—isn't it? At least,
THANK YOU FOR SHOPPING AT BORDERS.
WE WILL BE CLOSING IN FIFTEEN MINUTES.
thank God, we live in a day and age
where people aren't afraid to talk about orgasms.
Speaking of which, you've got to go see
the Orphée that just opened at Performers' Collective.
All the actors have been in car crashes,
and they've added an orgy—it's a little derivative,
but what isn't, these days? OK, got to run,
ciao, I'll see you later, love to all.
THANK YOU FOR SHOPPING AT BORDERS.
WE WILL BE CLOSING IN FIFTEEN MINUTES.

THANK YOU FOR SHOPPING AT BORDERS.
WE WILL BE CLOSING IN FIFTEEN MINUTES.

III. BALLAD OF THE POLICE DEPARTMENT

"Loving a music man ain't always
what it's supposed to be," she thought
as the fang pierced her heel and she sank.
This is the song of love and the law,
of what is enduring and what disappears.

Dissolving, her eye met its twin in the water
(or was it a glass in the guise of a stream?)
In the cafe, the boys drank to Orpheus.
Encircled by drafts on the tables and floor,
he waved a half-wave and lit a Gitane.

Sirens we were used to, but so early?
Through a window specked by last night's rain,
I saw Wojohowicz give him the news,
then returned to my book: *The Invention of Chance*.
This is the song of atomic decay.

Contemporary fascination
with corporal preservation
recapitulates the ancient
ceremonies of atonement,
or so, at least, it seems to me,
as I lecture empty rooms
on F. H. Bradley and the moon.
Not the moon you lovers see,
the moon as it appears to me
and me alone, my eyes refined
by distillation in the mind.
My moon rains light through long night hours
awake within the prison tower
of internal experience,
the tower holding thief and prince,
stockbroker and the child of fame,
identically, but not the same.
One hears the scraping of the key.
One wishes one were one, not me.

Through darkness he descended to the platform.
One quarter struck another. Buskers
danced in supplication of the shadows,
mirroring the disgraced King of Pop.
White noise announced the train. Orpheus wept.

After North and Clybourn comes Division,
and after Division, the final law, whose lord
sits anxiously beside his stolen bride.
I will not pretend I know the song he sang
before the dreadful pair. You know the stories

as well as I: that from the gramophone
a swell of scratch and hurl and gem-like glint,
of vouchsafed soul and breakbeats reconciled,
shattered the shale resolve of Death himself:
edict turned to grace. But I can still

remind you of the lesson coming up,
paused as we are at the axis of our hope.
Necessity may, for a moment, yield to love,
but love explodes each moment in its drive
to the next, and the next, and the next, like footsteps—

With a sudden cry Sgt. Wojo averred:
"The song of policemen has yet to be heard!
You can call it ignoble, or even absurd,
But my comrades have hung on each sibilant word,
And we've waited and waited as locations blurred
From subway to Hades: we've yet to be heard!"
Amid shouts of sha-hoobla, tik-tak, and tra-lay,
The song of policemen now carried the day.
Brass buttons new polished, bright jackets fresh pressed,
And riot protectors protecting their chests,
From buses and wagons policemen erupted,
From storefronts and stations, and uninterrupted
They sang as they rounded up each interloper:
Each anti-war chanter, each car window soaper.
They sang like a city-sized 8-track recorder,
And phalanxed, Miranda'ed, preserved the disorder
That the bravest policeman felt clutch at his heart
From the untamed community begging his art.

"Hey-hey-o," they sang, and such pleasant palaver,
And then morning came. They were walking cadavers.
They might tell funny stories, or wrestle, or shout,
But something—divine spark? the soul?—had gone out.
And all of the people and all of the streets
And all of the sweet shops where young lovers meet
Invisibly withered, and no one could say
Where the deadness had come from, how long it might stay.
But now Wojohowicz regrets his decision
To insert himself. There will be no revision.
So he takes off his hat and he gives up his gun
And that's how the song of policemen is done.

Where were you then?
            I was at North and Clybourn.

No one was with you?
            I was alone.

And Death's dispensation?
            It came with conditions.

Conditions you flouted?
            I slipped. The underworld does not forgive.

When all aloud the wind is blowing,
    And coughing drowns the poet's song,
And terminals brood softly glowing,
    And Marian wears a blue sarong,

When synthecrabs squirm in the beaker,
Then nightly hums the opaque speaker
       Tu-who;
Tu-whit, tu-who—a subtle note,
While Joan stirs on in a distant plot.

Arm. The words of Mercury are oddly muted after the studies
    of Jessie Weston. You, that way: we, this way.

IV. GAZA STRIP

       A current under sea
Picked his bones in whispers. And this I know.
Forgot the way of gulls. He rose and fell.
His teeth as white as snow.

A current under sea. O you
Walk her every day into the deep sea swell.
She passed the stages of her age and youth.
Orpheus wept. A big big love.

O you who turn the wheel,
Consider how his bones were picked,
A fortnight dead. And this I know.
Gentile or Phoenician, dark Don Juan,
A big big love. A big big love. As tall as you.

V. DEATH TO POETRY

Orpheus awoke in the poem of disguises, the poem once called "The Waste Land." Friends, listen up. He gathered the remnants of the life he had dreamed. He renounced the burden of the name he bore. He began to walk.

Orpheus walked down Milwaukee Avenue toward the Flatiron Building. He passed bodegas, taquerias, vintage stores. He met a hustler with a gas can. He walked past the anarchist kids. And he walked, and he walked, and he walked past the cabdrivers trading insults in Urdu, and he walked past convenience stores, and he walked past Latin Kings, and he walked past waitresses getting off night shifts, and he walked past jazz stars that nobody recognized, he walked past the students, the teachers, the cops. And the sky was the color of eggplant and tire fires, the sky was the field that resisted exhaustion. And he walked, and he walked past the puddles and gutters. And no one walked with him. And SUVs burned, and the asphalt ran liquid and Orpheus saw the dissolving sky and he knew that the name of the poem he had entered could not be "The Waste Land" or even "White Phosphorus," or "The Song of Policemen." In his pocket he fingered a tiny slip of paper. He opened and read it. It said, "This is the death of the poet." And yes. And yes. This is the death of the poet.

Shhhh. I am allergic to melodrama.

Shhhh. The serpent encircles the world.

Shhhh. There is a plausible explanation.

But watch it! the daughters of Ismara,
Their heaving chests wrapped up in beastly fleece,
From their hilltop perch, catch sight of Orpheus
Smithing his voice to match plucked strings.
Cunctaque tela forent cantu mollita, sed ingens
Clamor et infracto Berecyntia tibia cornu
Typanaque et plausus et Bacchei ululatus
Obstrepuere sono citharae, tum denique saxa
Non exauditi rubuerunt sanguine vatis.
And the stones grew red with the blood of the poet.
These footnotes have I shored against my ruins.
These footnotes
                    shhhh
                              we set foot
in a world ash-sick, a bad dream world
no longer the mirror, no longer the poem

the birdless night grew colder

And once the poem ended, commentary began. I said, I, the
author, said, "Orpheus is a mask in a poem infected with masks."
I said, "The importance of footnotes cannot be overestimated."
I said, "The essential problem of the poem is the essential
problem of our time, of all time: how to love one another." And
I was not, readers, Orpheus, and I did not descend into the
depths, and I have only these words to defend me, and the
shadows, the shadows howl for my blood

Once more in the city he refused to name
a phenomenon that I have often noticed
Once more in the city that endures its fall
Well then Ile fix you. Mackie's back in town
Once more in the city called Barnes and Noble
an elaborate deception, like a bird
Once more in the city that everyone forgot
and swerved to catch the sun on its wing
cf. McGinty, Possum Among the Hoopoes
a broken face, a city of dust and telescopy
abandoned the ruse that had once been the poem
and listened as the buildings lightly sang:

       Oh we'll meet again
       When all the rained out faces
       And all the bomb-scarred places
       Kiss me kiss me kiss me
       Under the telegraphic moon
       And I won't get up, I won't
       Get up, I'll never, never, never

OTHER POEMS

SUMMER OF LOVE

I bought a new red sweatsuit
to keep myself in the game.
It worked like the worst kind of music.
Birds kept flying past my head.
I skipped my dentist appointment.

Eventually
I thought I'd meet up
with the visions all those poets
promised. You know who I'm
talking about: William Carlos Williams,

Edgar Cayce, Mr. C. W. Post.
Broken rhymes for a broke-down time.
At night we'd roll the ice cream man
down his wooden slide

and lock him up inside
his broke-down ice cream house.
We didn't try to pry out all his secrets,
but drove away, hardly noticing the snow.

J. BEER 1969-1969

It was when they determined that I had been born dead
That my life became easier to understand. For a long time,
I wondered why rooms felt colder when I entered them,
Why nothing I said seemed to stick in anyone's ear,
Frankly, why I never had any money. I wondered
Why the cities I walked through drifted into cloud
Even as I admired their architecture, as I pointed out
The cornerstones marked "1820," "1950." The only songs
I ever loved were filled with scratch, dispatches from
A time when dead ones like me were a dime a dozen.
I spent my life in hotels: some looked like mansions,
Some more like trailer parks, or pathways toward
A future I tried to point to, but how could I point,
With nothing but a hand no hand ever matched,
With fingers that melted into words that no one read.

I rehearsed names that others taught me: Caravaggio,
Robert Brandom, Judith, Amber, Emmanuelle Cat.
I got hungry the way only the dead get hungry,
The hunger that launches a thousand dirty wars,
But I never took part in the wars, because no one lets
A dead man into their covert discussions.
So I drifted from loft to cellar, ageless like a ghost,
And America became my compass, and Europe became
The way that dead folks talk, in short, who cares,
There's nothing to say because nobody listens,
There's no radio for the dead and the pillows seem

Like sand. Let me explain: when you're alive,
As I understand it, pillows cushion the head, the way
A lover might soothe the heart. The way it works for me,
In contrast, is everything is sand. Beds are sand,
The women I profess to love are sand, the sound of music
In the darkest night is sand, and whatever I have to say
Is sand. This is not, for example, a political poem,
Because the dead have no politics. They might have
A hunger, but nothing you've ever known
Could begin to assuage it.

THE PASTE MAN

You'd better have an adhesive kind of mind
if you want to keep up with global fluctuations
in the quality of sound: a sudden irruption
of rain sound, say, from a dull red canopy
across the street from Frank's place, one single
shot in the night, foot pulled from muck,
tape hiss. The slippery dusk conspires
to keep you one step behind yourself.
Delivery trucks disguise themselves as chandeliers,
recede into the ceiling with a barely audible
click!, sealing you off from their treats,
radical news or fruit juice combinations.
At the Commercial Museum a man's super-glued
to the sky. He can see you right now.
You look like a speck of confetti
careless sweepers left behind in the convention aftermath.

FLOWERS

We got to the pier just as the boat was pulling away.
In the distance, a single cloud glowered. The air
Felt like sand, although it remained
Breathable. We walked

Back through town, where the parade
Was still beginning. Five high school bands
Marched by, each playing "Tangerine"
In microtonal variations. I wanted

A pretzel. While my back was turned,
The unicorns passed, silent, side
By side, just like they do in ancient drawings.
I didn't see a single one.

Afterwards, Amber reminded me
To tell her all the poems she figured in.
I made an Excel chart, including "Lucinda,"
"The Waste Land," "Globe," and some others

She'd never heard of. "I hate all those poems,"
She said. "You promised you'd write a poem
About the time we got to the pier
Just as the boat was pulling away. You promised,
But you never did."

SWIFT BOAT VETERAN FOR BEAUTY

The mission, when we finally arrived,
seemed paler, more insubstantial
than in the travel agent's glowing description.
More muck, less hacienda. Let me be the first
to underscore the insignificance of lineage.
And where did you get that handkerchief, again?
At the handkerchief shop. Little Batson sold me it.
Twelve men approached him as he sang
the song of the lovely wanderer, transposed
into a key I suddenly found unfamiliar.
The men deny that they are lonely.
Their tears speak out against them, even if
they explain it away as antifreeze residue
or hints of the mist that surrounds us.
By the side of the road: three shoes.

And where did you get that handkerchief, again?
She replied, "Pianos have been known to lose their tune
when played by antic hands." Understand me:
I didn't take this as an answer, or I probably shouldn't have,
and wouldn't, if I weren't as feeble
as everyone suspected, and prone to jawing on
long after the mouse had fled my trap.
This isn't my apartment: I won't sleep here for long.
Tomorrow I'll return to wandering
through the halls of the house I have stolen
from children I don't expect to ever see.

TOTAL INFORMATION AWARENESS

"This bubble had to be burst, & the only way to do it was
to go right into the heart of the Arab world
& smash something." The hotel heiress, snapped
flashing her bum in a Bahamas club.

To go right into the heart of the Arab world,
they claim their device can trigger an orgasm:
flashing her bum in a Bahamas club
on a boozy date with her new bloke, Nick Carter.

They claim their device can trigger an orgasm.
American officials who spoke on condition of anonymity
on a boozy date with her new bloke, Nick Carter,
say he confessed under torture in Syria.

American officials who spoke on condition of anonymity
without touching a woman's genital area
say he confessed under torture in Syria.
"There's no explanation why. We're just not saying anything."

Without touching a woman's genital area,
I take it all seriously. I am withdrawing from all representation.
There's no explanation why. We're just not saying anything
to make this objective absolutely clear.

I take it all seriously. I am withdrawing from all representation,
but he was in the special removal unit.
To make this objective absolutely clear,
the development of counterterrorism technologies—

but he was in the special removal unit.
This had profoundly shocked the commission,
the development of counterterrorism technologies
with the flick of a switch. Women get turned on.

This had profoundly shocked the commission.
No one detected any radical political views.
With the flick of a switch, women get turned on
to a new business model that only pretends

no one detected any radical political views.
I take it all seriously. I am withdrawing from all representation
to a new business model that only pretends
to give consumers more control. In fact,

I take it all seriously. I am withdrawing from all representation
that she refused to be photographed in body paint
to give consumers more control. In fact,
he was handcuffed and beaten repeatedly.

That she refused to be photographed in body paint
constitutes an integral goal of the IOA.
He was handcuffed and beaten repeatedly.
There's no explanation why. An information whiteout

constitutes an integral goal of the IOA
while Justice turns to Syria's secret police.
There's no explanation why. An information whiteout.
Forebodings of disaster enter into box scores

while Justice turns to Syria's secret police,
constructing systems to counter asymmetric threats.
Forebodings of disaster enter into box scores
to achieve total information awareness,

constructing systems to counter asymmetric threats.
This bubble had to be burst, and the only way to do it was
to achieve total information awareness
& smash something. The hotel heiress snapped.

BOB HOPE IS NOT A PLAN

What was I trying to get at? Once posed in that condition,
the question seemed slightly insane, a septet of cardinals
lunching at the Rainforest Café. The old skin issues
kept reasserting themselves, a wayward boomerang
lurching hither and yon, over hills and dales and hibernating
bears. The investigating committee requested
that I stick more closely to the script, wipe the pie
from my eye, all the usual bullshit. I complied.
Then I went for a five-mile hike. In the clear cool of dawn,
or in the aimless atmosphere of noon, or maybe even
in twilight's hungry cloak, I came across
a set of golden steak knives next to a sign. The sign read,
"These Are Not Your Father's Steak Knives." But I knew
deep down it lied: these knives were my father's, and his
     father's
before him, all the rueful way down to lizards and muck.

FLOWERS

We got to the pier just as the boat was pulling away.
In the distance, a pair of clouds glowered.
Now the train was our only hope. But it was
Miles away, in a part of town we didn't know.

"I think we should take a rickshaw," I said.
"A rickshaw?" "Yes, a rickshaw. How else
Can we avoid the holiday crowds?
How else can we pass through

This city's cruel gates and its checkpoints?
Don't forget the octagonal marketplace."
Minutes later, Amber and I
Wheeled past the flower vendors' stalls

To arrive at the station. Elsewhere
In the city, unicorns processed
In single file, as the legends promise.
A policeman stopped us. Briskly, he asked,

"Do you know where you are?"
I looked at Amber. She said, "We arrived
In this city without knowing its name.
We wanted the boat, but we missed it.

Now we need to take the train."
He looked at us with bemusement.
"Take the train? take the train?
There's no train to take."

TRAPPED IN THE CLOSET

I love you: the first lesson
gunplay teaches. I find my breath
under the table, a tourniquet
not needed at the moment.
I open my eyes and the wall bleeds you.

Everyone dreams big these days.
For instance, universal war,
or grab a massive advance
on a memoir about growing up
in a family of bankers,

trusting in quiet accumulation
of capital, as though that's
a natural fact. Was it really me
under the table? I couldn't be sure,
but I knew my leg hurt a hell of a lot.

Everyone dreams of love, why not?
I'm no different from you,
even if I take strange pride in my beard,
the way a couple of gray strands
seem to announce a certain challenge

met: we both made it this far.
Out by the beach the jets are keeping
us safe. It only burns for a second,
this composure, this disease
we accept as the cost of ourselves.

GLOBE

for Amber Sutherland

There are many things in this world,
and one of them is you. Others include
icicles, cupcakes, doorknobs, skulls,
and little dogs with bad attitudes.
Giraffes lick walls, and dolphins
lick giraffes: the natural world
is simply what it is. We go along
resenting jerks who tell us what to do
or signal lane changes at the last
possible minute. "I suspect
there's something wrong with your chin."
Policemen drift in, ticket me
for no seatbelt, and then their day
is done. You've been a ghost,
a nymphet, you've advised supermodels,
you fend off table audits. All these things
are you, or colored by you. Recently
I order too much coffee while you sleep.
Icicles are the perfect murder weapon.
Cupcakes are what's needed on your birthday,
exactly three of them. Metaphor is what a life
becomes while waiting for direction:
the target makes the vehicle expand.
Where you leave your lettered purse,
a rabbit and cat follow. Call it
Australia or Vermont, a tower
by a lake, a pony revolution,

a story filled with aging hipster dreams.
All of these things are yours, or something
like them. I got this globe for you.

LIVES OF THE POETS

No angel but goes into the ground. I found myself
walking along the side of an enormous spaceship.
"I have heard that you combine the pride of lions
with a certain aversion to laundry," the lead man said.
What could I do but agree? The sky flashed
a green ampersand. Nothing is new.
I had a hankering for peanuts, for salt
solid in the mouth. Somewhere underneath
a river carved out a course for future
subterranean trains.
                        Alice cannot understand
the language except by holding secret cards
close to the expanse of her oracular breast.
Alice doesn't see her death as tragic.
While she collapsed, I was auditioning
for the part of the Fool in a play I called
"The Fool." There were two other characters:
Stepfool and the vicious Nightwalker.
I expect the run to be long and profitable.

FLOWERS

We got to the pier but the boat never came.
The sky was as blue as it gets. Around seven,
A single star came out. We decided
To try and find a restaurant.

We walked down the city's broad, inspiring
Avenues. All around us, traces of the afternoon's
Parade: popcorn kernels in the gutters,
Birds carrying broken balloons.

We found a place with an Irish theme.
Amber ordered a Top o' the Mornin'.
I had the corned beef soufflé. Our server asked
If we'd seen the unicorns, but we

Ignored her. "The people here are strange,"
Amber said. "I wish we were on a boat right now,
Heading for the capital. They said the boat
Has a disco." "It has a disco and a casino,

And when you're hungry, they serve sandwiches,"
I said. "You're making fun of me."
"I'm not—you'll see tomorrow. It has to come
Tomorrow." We paid the bill and left.

SPEAK YON UNDISCOVERED TOWERS

Remember how we ran across each other
Waiting on the L train, in hot Williamsburg?
I had some undeveloped photographs
With which I planned to establish
The reign of light, ten thousand years
Of light. I couldn't quite explain

How one and one makes two, it's
A postulate, nobody's interested, there's
No profits in houses or anything but
War, forever, and girls shipped over the border
From Moldavia to Oslo, from villages
On the fringes of Chiang Mai to Yonkers

And to San Francisco and everywhere that
Poetry, unwished for, flourishes,
A disease of language, while meanwhile
I left my papers on the airplane. Did you
Find them yet? I have a lot to prepare for,
Repent for, no cats in this vicinity,

Slow music is the worst kind of music,
The world I speak for can never exist,
But Shelley already took care of that,
Yeah, Shelley and Charles Bernstein and whoever,
And no one saw the fires on the towers,
What towers? It was good to see you.

NO ONE HERE GETS OUT ALIVE:
THE LIFE OF LEE HARVEY ELIOT

Something happens. The idea is
to keep people from catching on fire.
"It smells so nice in here, like it's
some kind of castle." Why else would I
have scattered my favorite propositions
in the path of some angry loser,
destined for at least a couple of minutes
to fill the day with mist, turn trumpets
into a series of abstract paintings
called "Abstract Series"? The part
about mythology is finally over.
What replaced it nobody could say,
but giggled shyly, like a young
farmgirl, and proclaimed to his class,
"Flee to the mountains, for the end
of all things is at hand!" He was acting
as a safety valve, keeping the two young lovers
from becoming overheated. Good luck!
Eliot had a secretary named Pound,
Pound a secretary named Mussolini.
(Capsule history of the twentieth
century.) Well, come on, I mean
some of my best friends are modernists,
or were, before their education fell upon them,
devouring hearts and livers, leaving
bare ruined backpacks behind. The more
there is to see, the less there is to say
about it, except for maybe, "Look at the view,"

"I fell on account of the pretzel," or
"The wine I wanted to buy
wasn't there any more." Meanwhile
an interminable series of internal conflicts
play themselves out, like single trumpeters
along a winding Spanish alley. It
promises to be an arduous night,
and then it finds its promise
impossible to keep, but at the last
it finds its promise, writes it in flashes
across the pale pink sky:
Flee to the mountains!
The end of all things is at hand!

THESES ON FAILURE

1. I wanted to announce the chief defect of red. I wanted to decline the works of the Acme Cooperative. I wanted to say something important—no, something profound—no, something by which you might remember me. Why was I unable? Why was my eye distracted by a photograph?

According to the photograph, Feuerbach wants a big bowl of pasta. He does not want to think of a big bowl of pasta, he wants to have it in front of him. He wants the thing itself. But Feuerbach forgets. He forgets. He forgets. He forgets the origins of pasta. Hence, in *Das Wesen des Christenthums*, he writes with a brush of human hair. You told me that I couldn't translate "Das Wesen des Christenthums" as "Christian Thumbways." You said it was too dumb. I filed this thesis under failure to apply the method.

2. I got home and you were already gone. A note on the table:

"The question whether objective truth can be attributed to human thinking is not a question of theory but is a practical question. Man must prove the truth—i.e. the reality and power, the this-sidedness of his thinking in practice. The dispute over the reality or non-reality of thinking that is isolated from practice is a purely scholastic question."

A big bowl of pasta overturned on the floor. In the back yard our ladder surrounded by corpses.

This thesis is not invisible as it ought to be. Pray for it. Pray for it, my love.

3. Where was the school, and why did the school keep calling us? You say, "Circumstances are changed by men." You say, "It is essential to educate the educator himself." Then you begin to show me the photos.

"Why is my face blacked out of these?"

"Acme Processing did it," you say. "I won't go there again."

Filosofove svet jen ruzne vykladuli.

Carelessness. Sloth. Indifference.

4. I know how you feel about dream narratives. Nevertheless.

5. I am walking across our porch, littered with anvils and giant rubber bands. Inside our anniversary party. Your mother argues with Charles Bernstein, framed by shark jaws. It is snowing in August, so I know we must be back in Buffalo.

You tell me they're ruining our party, and the candles are already lit. You tell me I have to do something. But I'm too engrossed in the book—it's *Christian Thumbscrews*, and I read, "After the earthly family is discovered to be the secret of the holy family, it must be destroyed in theory and in practice." I am holding a flaming light-saber.

My shoulder hurts. I whisper to Charles Bernstein, "You know, a lot of men make jokes about their mothers-in-law, but we have a great relationship." He takes the crown from my head. I start to ascend the ladder.

I want to put this thesis under "accident." But I know there are no accidents.

6. In his pamphlet, *Das Wesen der Menschlichkeit*, Feuerbach imagines an infinite series of photographs. Each image, he writes, is implied by the one that follows it, so that the viewer gradually retraces the interior history of the world. The eleventh, for instance, depicts a child gazing after the balloon she has released. The twelfth shows an industrial spy lurking outside the balloon factory. The thirteenth—do I need to continue?

I am not writing these theses to explain anything.

Except Feuerbach never mentions the corpses.

Filosofove svet jen ruzne vykladuli.

The point is

7. O, I scheduled filming at the factory gates. The typists emerged, women in frocks, men in plain black coats, and look! look at the wind made visible as it ripples through the crowd. I arranged a spectacle for your living eye, you who outrun me, you whose course I cannot predict. How cruel the logic of self-education!

I set out to write a treatise on failure, and it turned out my subject was love. Call it my confusion. One catches oneself, inevitably, in the trap set for the speeding bird. What renders the rent net holy.

8. "All social life is essentially practical."

In other words, don't touch me.

9. "Your main problem is you never want to do anything."

"Your problem is you live your life in the abstract."

And when I got to the field, you were already gone. I turned off the engine and went out to see the stars. What can I say about stars that hasn't been said already? They are small and various and if each is a world, they are mostly, mostly dead and cold. They pale beside the moral law within. They pale beside what you and I have made.

This thesis relates the shame of the actor with respect to the script.

This thesis is the song of embarrassment.

10. So I called you to say my battery went dead. Later I learned the mundane truth: I'd caught you at the dinner table, you and Feuerbach, sharing pasta garnished with acorn squash. But at the time I couldn't interpret your words, the hint of recovered birdsong I'd lost or never had.

Professor Gypsum: "Each of us is composed of a nested set of cages, the mother beside her imprisoned offspring. Culture promised us that descendants might liberate their ancestors, ignorant of barbs, unharrowed by the cunning of topology. But the word is a tetter. If you, my prize students, examine the illustration, you will observe, I trust, that what you took for your most intimate feelings could only have been part of a larger pattern of oblivion. Sad emus, gnawing at the branch! Sad systems of logistic, able to compass all truth within their finite axiomatization only on pain of welcoming the false as well! I would rather be a stone than a professor, weeping erosive non-tears, accepting final weather."

Professor Magnet: "Consider red and the word 'red.' Is this the failure of language, or of color, or do you reject the question? I walked from Leningrad to Prague for you, under one arm a ladder, under the other a taxonomy of vegetables. On the road to Bukovina, I fell to the ground. When I arose I saw nothing."

Professor Nembutol: "What can I know? What may I hope for? Please help me, for I have forgotten. Forgotten my name, forgotten my address, forgotten the color of my coat. Hail you forgotten, mother of cages. Have something. Have something for me."

11. Philosophers have only interpreted the world.

The point is to change it.

It will not be changed.

SONNETS TO MORPHEUS

"I know kung fu." It won't bring back the world.
5:15 a.m.: I wake from another dream,
the same as every dream. A man builds a ship
in my chest. Each of the sailors
carries by her breast a picture of her sister.
The ship is not the image of a ship.
Beyond its sails there are no stars.
The water is only water because it's black.

5:15 a.m. Perhaps you've seen me
practicing my moves in the empty prison yard
and wondered whether you were the dreamer
conjuring me into existence from the bare
desire to caress a phantom ship
and my death the death of your desire.

Listen, I want to tell you about Trinity.
I spent last night in a graveyard. I could hear
grass grow like hair. My love held back my kit.
I woke up bald. Edgar Poe
wrote a story that predicted it: "Lenore."
The dead return and we don't recognize them.
I woke up with wounds on my chest and shoulders.
"And then I saw the fields with my own eyes."

Listen, I'm trying to warn you about milk.
You're not the only customer. I began
to write my letter on the train to winter,
the last long winter train. Now I know
that I was born to sail. It's 5:15,
reportedly. The grass grew thick and hot.

Relentless self-preservation eats us away:
ghosts confront ghosts at car shows,
aquarium benefits, banks, a midnight flick.
And yet bliss it remained to be alive
in that gray dusk—to run a finger
along your cunning spine, match wits
with Leeza Gibbons, watch T. Scholz
clamber to the roof. "There are two ways

out of this building." Suppose he knows
the choice before the scenery appears.
Let's say our final fight is choreographed
nine months before I take you down
in a dumpster-heavy alley. Still I pack
my travel kit, rehearse a chilly word.

Today's another sad and lonesome day.
I try to count my friends. Then I see
the old songs have a point. "Stop trying
to hit me and hit me." So keep in mind
the void where things begin. In New Orleans
a man in a pinstripe suit buys a Z-Speed
industrial vibrator, perfect for sand or plastic.
Even for special effects. I dream of tigers.

I went to Bangkok for business purposes.
In the stillness, someone follows me.
A licorice advertisement: "Make your mouth
attain to the fourteenth level." I've been training
my mind and body for a moment just like this,
studying lives of the saints and of the assassins.

What did you have to hope for? A single sun
reflected in swamp water, in
a building's silver skin. "You don't know
what it is, but it's there, like a splinter
in your mind." Blank checks
pile up in the mailbox. Lunchtime:
singers in grey hats, ambling past
the statue from your first dream. Don't look back.

It's the same exact sun you saw as a kid.
I looked it up already. Everything else
starts slithering across your field of vision.
My flight to Bangkok leaves at 5:15.
I pack a pair of scissors in my bag,
a photograph, an apple, *Leaves of Grass*.

People collapse like dominoes. All roads
lead to Wells and Lake. My task:
develop a metaphysics of song
and commit myself to it. My teacher
hovers slightly to the left of the screen.
She knows I cannot know what I have seen:
the city has a freedom that evades
our clumsy harnesses, its blues and reds

resist sight's tyranny, its pheromones
soak into commuters languid in the cave.
And children shyly turn against my words.
The rising I predicted comes to pass
before I'm there. "Sounds to me like you might
need to unplug, man." Bodies collapse.

I can't say how I ended up in Bangkok.
What time is it? Depression assumes
its latest form: a taste for blood.
You have to believe in a better world
hidden within the glitzy architecture,
not quite outside of time, but radiant,
unmediated, yoga-like, pristine.
The ghost of a pallid hunter met my gaze.
My dollar rejected by the vending machine.

"Don't tell me you're a believer now." Not quite.
I'm abandoning the neutral clothing, though.
Can't say for sure what year it is. The airport's
thick with signs: dervishes, T1
connection posts clustered like mass graves,
a black fleck steady in my swamp-green eye.

"Remember, all I'm offering is the truth."
For instance, on March 1, 2005,
_____ die, _____ remain jailed,
or you appear for the first time.
I'd like to consider the meal we shared
or your face framed by the falling snow,
but my mind was stuffed with names and photographs
and had no room for your unending pain.

Fate took over.
It's not as though I drank your blood
exactly. But here's what I wrote:
"for business purposes" "it's 5:15"
while something inside of you gleams
as if a door into the earth had opened.

An expansive spirit, wasted, shames
the vistas of its youth: the girl
who lifted up her brittle map of Thailand
to explain that "geopolitics" eluded her,
as though we were ever free from tactics
or cartography. "I need guns.
Lots of guns." The children line up
beside the pond. They never realize

we poison them with their own reflected breath.
We gesture at fake horses,
trace lines in the mud, houses collapse,
streets grow impassable, livestock decays,
awkwardness replaces ecstasy,
padlocked the playgrounds, sand in the cake.

Their music fell into my heart
like an unexpected taxi. So what
if you're a god. You're not immune to starving,
once the world decides your voice is innocent.
"Buckle your seatbelt, Dorothy. Kansas
is going bye-bye." Last night I swam
through the gates of Chalk City. Why did you insist
I take up this power over you?

The power to declare, "My token's worthless.
The life I live is the only possible life.
Here is a handful of snow. Here's an infant.
Here's the purest animal, a tooth
embedded in a nipple." So I bit
to prove I'm more than the sum of my mirrors.

Unveiling, that's the stuff. I leave
a glass of wine on the table. Ten days later
it's still a glass of wine. I'm not myself.
A glass of wine the color of nebulae.
"Your men are already dead." We were warned,
elsewhere, and shouldn't blame the objects:
blue bottles, skin, your hand without a ring.
I traveled to Bangkok for business purposes.

A truck could snap his spine in half. Still he'd rage
to whisper the truth in a last gargling breath.
Nothing stops him: insidious drugs or robots run amok.
Out-dreaming the ones who dreamt being into being,
he hopes us along. In Bangkok, I'm trying to say,
I looked in a mirror and nothing looked back.

"This line is tapped, so I must be brief."
I've already said more than I was supposed to,
spilled words like bullets onto rainy pavement,
coughed them up like milk. So now they're yours.
Don't forget to thank the little dog
who catches your eye when you suddenly look up:
you've had enough of reading about how things are,
decide you want to have a look for yourself.

But don't expect him to thank you in return.
He wanders off past the vegetable stands. The air
gets thick and hot. Can you really
breathe yourself into existence, touch the world,
and still leave behind a path for another to see?
Nobody told you to come here. There's nobody here.

THE PERFUMED CRYPT

OR

FOUR QUARTERS IN EIGHT BITS

I. CAUGHT UP IN THE RAPTURE

It begins with a dream.
Armand Petitjean dreams of giving women
the most beautiful things possible.
He is obsessed by this dream.
It is 1935.
He cannot sleep or eat. He cannot even
work on sound films. Marcel Carné is furious.
Carné's film *Le Jour se lève* cannot be silent.
In this day and age the people want sound!
Petitjean doesn't care. He dreams only
of women and the beauty that they require.
His mind blazes with gems and bits of glass,
ostrich feathers, the moon, and water by night.
A somnambulist, he wanders out of Paris.
He walks along dusty roads, past farmers
in wooden clogs. He has not eaten
in weeks. Nothing matters to him.
In the cafés, Marcel Carné weeps to Jean Cocteau.
The film is at a standstill!
Petitjean isn't quite sure what district he's come to.
His face is grimy, his hair matted with sweat.
He shuffles one foot in front of the other.
A glorious vision hovers before his uncertain eyes:
a ruined château. From the wall of the castle
grows a lush, blood-red rose. He sees the rose
from a hundred yards away. It reminds him
of beauty, and that reminds him of women.
He silently sobs. In later years
he sometimes claimed that a dark hand put out

the candles on the altar, or that a hidden voice
whispered a question to him, but no trace
of such events is found in published accounts.
Regardless, Petitjean dedicated himself
from that day on to the pursuit of beauty,
symbolized by the rose,
the emblem of his new company: Lancôme.

With the smell of hyacinths across the garden
I can smell the different perfumes,
The smell whereof shall breed a plague in France,
And smell renews the salt savour of the sandy earth
And rain, the blood-rose living in its smell,
With smell of steaks in passageways,
I mean of taste, sight, smell, herbs, fruits, and flowers,
The closed-in smell of hay. A sumac grows
In the smell of grapes on the autumn table
About her daunst, sweet flowers, that far did smell
Of the smell of apples and lemons, of the pairing of birds.
Excellent! I smell a device.

So I asked the students, both men and women, what was their
sense of old people? "They don't smell good," one answered.
"They ramble on." "They can't take care of themselves. No one
understands what they're talking about and they look awful." I
couldn't say anything. I was a creature of words, obsolete in the
frenzy of images dominating their minds. And wasn't I, really,
starting to smell a little strange, of dust and violets with a sour
undertone? Wasn't I starting to ramble on, make my listener's

eyes glaze over, catch at sleeves in order to sketch out intricate descriptions of cities I only imagined? Every fresh tangent that seized me with a need to elaborate started to feel like sand in my throat, like a confession of irrelevance, just one more aging talker whose audience is captive only until the final grades are posted, and whose revenge on the evaluations comes swiftly, even as I pointed out to deans and to committees the statistical futility, the unreliability of such measures, the majestic summation of a thousand minor errors and inaccuracies into an enormous diversion, a scarlet herring demanding genuflection even as it led us away from whatever ideals were meant to orient us in our work, but who after all can blame them when it's only the microcosm following the macrocosm, each local flabbiness merely the sign of a greater glut, and all the various defenses assumed by young and old alike just a reflex response to a civilizational process larger than anyone can quite discern, touching almost in their inefficacy, like putting on sunglasses before the mushroom cloud. Plus I'd gotten your message right before class.

At the gala that evening Lindsay Owen-Jones, CEO of the L'Oréal group, and Marc Menesguen, International CEO of Lancôme, were surrounded by many prestigious guests including: Inès Sastre, Cristiana Reali and Marie Gillain of course, as well as many others . . .

I saw the table and it was me.
The people came. Faces.
An apron evoked fresh accumulation.

Can I name the other sausages? Dark,
Shabby mouths, pink puppets.
The rain somewhere isn't gathering.

I repeated a quiet. Here, there,
His face filled the school.
Our rules hesitated, sitting.
On a pocket, rusty and drifting,
Things let the years help,
But another curtain drops. Two gentle coils.

Although I disappointed all the coins,
They put children on fruit. Puts paint
On urgent kisses. Things we used asleep.
Time for being sometimes followed.
Which wrapper comes to stare, to stare
And count the women, gaze and break?

I saw the window and it was gray.
Her slender streetcar came. "Good-bye,"
My coffee hissed. Can I make
The quarters good? Revive the babble?
Outside would find only a pocket.
Rest rested. The blue my letters.

II. PARADE GROUNDS

Dear Rose,

I know you must be angry, but there are exculpating reasons. I will show them to you tonight. Meet me at the corner of Russell and Ostend. I have so many beautiful things to show you, my darling. Life is inexhaustible.

Dear Core Brands Inc:

I waited for you last night by Ebertplatz. The night was windy and cold; I give it two thumbs down. You must hear that sort of thing a lot. Furthermore, you accused me in your several text messages of being uninformed about the world we live in, blindly following the lead of the mass media, und so weiter. But get this, mister: as I stood at the forsaken corner, waiting vainly for your step, I saw a ghostly procession thread the narrow streets. I saw a line of pilgrims draped in white linen, merchants in fine silk robes with jewelry from Persia and fine hats from the Indus valley, monks swaying in their sackcloth, and then a long line of children passed, none more than fifteen, each with his or her eyes fixed ahead. I called out to them, but no head turned. They looked as though they were meant for graves that they had dug themselves. It seemed like snow was falling on them; they turned the corner and were gone. I stood silent for a long time. Then I asked an old woman where the parade had come from, but she didn't understand me and hurried away. A soft perfume filled the air. Don't bother coming by tonight, you fake: you are not the champ of my heart.

The Explanation

Rose knew that her husband often met with a reporter
to discuss scandalous goings-on in the ship of state.
She didn't know why the actors were following her.

The man her husband met had been in the navy.
As a student, he had spent some months in Germany.
His partner was married to a famous screenwriter.

Knowing that her husband had affairs, the screenwriter
would often drink a pitcher of martinis
as she sat up watching the films of Marcel Carné.

Marcel Carné, the son of a cabinetmaker, worked
with Jacques Prévert on all his famous films, including
Le jour se leve, with sound by Armand Petitjean.

Le jour se leve was released in 1939. That year,
Heinrich Böll, after completing compulsory service,
enrolled at the University of Cologne.

The mayor of Cologne fled the town a few years later,
after taking part in the plot to assassinate Hitler.
He missed the Allied firebombing of his city.

The war was over. K. boarded a ship
for America. He only remembered the narrow streets
of his city in dreams. Now he made fake perfumes.

The actor thought he recognized the scent
that Rose was wearing. Each night he studied his lines
and every morning they melted away again.

Uma Thurman begins her role

When a pail is put out to despair,
I have empty hands. Sometimes
the dirt kills. Again.
Bodies of good, rest seized
nothing beyond the grinding men.
Bitter death must drain.

Often in watching, echoes of lipstick.
Yes, make so free a number.
So much outside, so ashamed by ringing
trains. How was the cost
announced? Thanks, dust.
My breath shook beet-red hymns.

Wind found the red as tall hands
swung, a cathedral.
Others carried God.
Down pockets of tuxedos, a black
figure stared. Not a life
in harmony. The children saw.

Attend a beaten noise, my wild
green crowd. Praise anchors.
Quiet Kafka, beaten in the quiet
corners, fished you out.

Nowhere slowly stood
beneath the red factory.

To hear, to touch, to taste, to smell, that's now
For the bent goldenrod and the lost sea-smell,
Each one with its peculiar and exciting smell.
Mine eyes smell onions; I shall weep anon.
I wake in the night and smell the trenches;
There is no use there is no use at all in smell, in teeth, in taste,
    in toast, in anything.
For the smell of water is but small,
And to smell, pah! like a flamingo,
And send a bad smell in,
The soul's sap quivers. There is no earth smell
Or smell of living thing. This is the spring time.
I have lost my sight, smell, hearing, taste, and touch.

III. DEATH BY FIRE

War falling on little balloons.
Was I the sick dancing? The tired
room? Drunk rubber
understood the overnight eyes.
Change in a nickel, a dark gaze
furious together.

Nothing moaning, realize,
conversations burn.
The search fell empty.
The voice, searching, slipped
in stupid grimy walls
and its terrible energy died.

All swayed. A chilly avenue
went up to the tavern.
Only a rhythm our hard hands
entered left. If I
had watched, I could apologize.
It's the name of dirt and prayers.

No folded reply. Narrow
absolution hissing. Can you
yearn to judge the visiting
day? Fifteen knocks
without a sudden child.
The street a crimson mirror.

This image of the multiplication of species that are usually suppressed in every possible way is a rare documentary record of life in a ravaged city. While the majority of the survivors may have been spared direct confrontation with the most repulsive fauna of the rubble, they were pursued everywhere by the flies at least, not to mention the stench of rotting and decay which, as Nossack writes, lay over the city.

On June 8th, Uma Thurman expressed this shared vision of beauty in Paris, before journalists from around the world, as well as at the gala that followed at the Hippodrome d'Auteuil.

Uma Thurman is a contemporary woman and sole master of her life.

Uma Thurman is about style.

The key to her success?

Her "passion for life."

As an actress, Uma Thurman is synonymous with versatility.

Uma Thurman definitely lives her life her way.

This combined with pure talent make Uma Thurman one of the hottest actresses of the 2000s.

Today Lancôme is offering this talented actress a brand new role.

Helping women the world over to share in the Lancôme vision.

"Believe in beauty."

Beauty of women who shine and are alive with energy.

Women who make a difference with a mere caress, a glance, a smile.

For the bent goldenrod and the lost sea-smell
Made sharp air sharper by their smell.
Feel the wind of it, smell the dust of it?
The spirits of the air live on the smells
Lured with the smell of infant blood, to dance
And shriek till at the smells of blood they stretch their
    bony wings—
They will not smell my fear, my fear, my fear.
I am stuffed, cousin; I cannot smell
And nothing but the very smell were left me.
Comforting smell breathed at every entering:
The smell of the wet feathers in the heat,
The smell of snow, stinging in nostrils as the wind lifts it from
    a beach,
Or pausing on high ground to smell the heather.

IV. SEARCH FOR TOMORROW

"Perfume, when you get right down to it,
is about fucking, just like death
is poetry's subject. That's why they're natural enemies,"
said the speaker, who kept carefully to the shadows.

The reporter took down notes in his little yellow pad.
"This is great stuff," he murmured, but he was only
half listening. He was thinking of the prizes to come,
the stables and the European skiing.

It was summer in the parking garage. Someone's dog
skidded into a post. A Frisbee followed.
The reporter drove home in his Subaru.
His wife had left a note on the kitchen counter.

Explanation Redux

Dear Bob,

The easiest way for me to tell you this is in the form of a
parable. A man wanted his company to sound authentic. He
wanted a name like Vendome or Francome. One of his assistants
had grown up in the Loiret district. As a child, he'd often seen
the local chateau, called Lancosme. The man liked the name,
and since he was an avid gardener, he made the rose his
company's symbol. A generation later, it had all become a story

of ruined castles, dark hands, and whispers. How does this relate to you? It's a parable, so draw your own conclusions. In the meantime, I've run off with Mr. K. At least he has the courage of his convictions, three for mail fraud, one for tax evasion.

In some sense, though, I'll always be your

Rose

The smell of witch-hazel indoors,
Shatterproof drinking glasses, the smell of kerosene,
Smell of green tea on Greene Street
(By any other name would smell as sweet),
Willows, the smell of the river, and a mass
On tips of thought where thoughts smell in the rain.
Nostalgia comes with the smell of rain, you know.
And from the flowers a sultry smell
Painted for sight, and essenced for the smell,
The exquisite smell of the earth at daybreak, and all through
    the forenoon
With grateful smell forth came the human pair.

Would any hands understand
the pendulum that changes
eating crumbs to goulash?
Machines advance, indelible brooding,
suffering, coins: the unstable age
couldn't see the coffin exactly.

Maybe I have a secret. I
couldn't leave until the dirty
conversation opened a crack
in the furniture, a ringing
sleep. It ended with
a donated melody.

It was slowly hoping
to indicate in the torn yellow air
that marriage
reached out to the delicate
factory, to the angry breath
love allowed.

Stop. Thirteen bedrooms,
two swans, a fire-blackened
coat. Only sometimes
meaning subsided.
God in my broken mouth.
Imagine them dancing without light.

MARY, COLOR SCIENTIST

Dieser Flucht folgt Eros, nicht Verfolger, sondern
als Liebender; dergestalt, daß die Schönheit um
ihres Scheines willen immer beide flieht: den
Verständigen aus Furcht und aus Angst den
Liebenden . . . Ob Wahrheit dem Schönen gerecht
zu werden vermag?

——Walter Benjamin

Our eye-beams twisted, and did thread
Our eyes, upon one double string.
——John Donne

blood in my eyes for you
——traditional

No one comes here anymore.
I have a token NO
I have an idea NO
I was washed up

on a lab table, in the traditional
manner. "Everybody wants
to say the joyful joyfully, and I
finally saw it, when I was destroyed."
Talk all you like, you're already dead.

**

Mary, would you like to come outside?
Mary worked so long and hard
In the palace of black and white.
Mary knows things I don't know.
She knows every tear I've cried.
She gave her life to seeing sight.
Mary, Mary, when will you come outside?

**

Well, we have these instruments

**

Beauty is a tooth. Correction:
The telephone rang. I was looking
At brown, there's a history
I'm not getting into, beauty
Is still a tooth. Correction:

Nobody wanted to go to the post office.

**

Individually a vision, a vision
Individuate. You manx.
"Yeah, it's that paper that lights up
When you look at it." But why did
The ground start moving? Catch up.
She knew it was happening before
It started to happen. Catch up.
"What did you do, pay for
Those eyes?"

**

Opaque: the rose is not red until your eyes fall upon it.

Translucent: the rose is not red until your eyes.

Transparent: the rose is not red.

**

Etc. Look, the story concerns Mary, and Mary alone. Mary
    alone in her colorless tower.
Snow will fall, day turn to night, and not even postmen evade
    her sight,
Lidless, fulfilling the ancient dream, she sees the tanks roll
    into Gaza
And dieters, she sees with all-encompassing eyes the shredding
    of orders,
Kids sneaking into *The Story of O*, the football scrimmage, and
    Manhattan
Ending, she sees the end of Paris and Fort Worth, she watches
    subways melt
Sleeplessly, she knew how it all would work out, she trains her
    dials on the death
Of kings sitting sadly by the waterfront shacks, she sees
    beyond the genius
Of Edwards Teller, Hopper, and Lear. You and I are the trouble
    she's seen.

Mary, wouldn't you like to come outside?

Mary, Mary, when will you come outside?

**

The sky was black. The sky was blue.
I was sitting someplace. I saw it.

**

The community got together, as communities will,
And waited together for death. Some of us
Were colorblind, so when they lifted the red flag
To signal the drink, we had to be prodded
By neighbors. In a couple of cases,
There were clusters of the colorblind, after all
A genetic trait: these familial bands
Required repeated prodding by strangers
On the outskirts. It produced a wavelike pattern,
All this prodding, so that to an outside observer,
One tuning in from remote satellite, for example,
It was reminiscent of a Busby Berkeley scene,
Or one of those marching band routines
In which the scrambling about of the sousaphone players
Suddenly blossoms into a starfish or some kind of
Risqué joke. But within fifteen minutes or so,
The prodding subsided, and after that the drinking,
The twitching, and we all lay dead in the field.

**

After she emerged, she saw red, and it was red.
She emerged, and saw yellow. She saw blue.
After she emerged, she saw what green was like.
She saw purple and orange and gray.

NOTES

Not only the title, but the plan and a good deal of the incidental symbolism of the book were suggested by the *Philosophical Investigations*. Indeed, so deeply am I indebted, Wittgenstein's book will elucidate the difficulties much better than my notes can do; and I recommend it (apart from the great interest of the work itself) to any who think such elucidation of my book worth the trouble. To another work of philosophy am I indebted in general, one which has influenced our generation profoundly; I mean Neil Strauss's *The Game: Penetrating the Secret Society of Pickup Artists*. I have used especially the techniques of "Real Social Dynamics," "Neuro-Linguistic Programming," and "Mystery Method." Anyone who is acquainted with these works will immediately recognize in my book certain references to vegetation ceremonies.

"Sound of Water Over a Rock"
Cf. Lax: "The first thing to do is admit your defeat. The first is admit your defeat."

"The Waste Land"
9: "Nobody could be less dogmatic or more obstinate than he. He relies entirely on his instinct." Re: Bresson.
10: V. Baudelaire, Preface to *Les Fleurs du Mal*.
12: They *are* assholes. A phenomenon that I have often noticed.
14: V. Journey, "Faithfully."
14: Max Gail was a teacher at the prestigious University Liggett School before becoming an actor. His acting debut came in 1970 at The Little Fox Theatre in San Francisco, California, playing Chief Bromden in the original stage production of

One Flew Over the Cuckoo's Nest. In 1973, he reprised this role in his New York stage debut.

15: F. H Bradley, *Appearance and Reality*, p. 346:
"My external sensations are no less private to myself than are my thoughts or my feelings. In either case my experience falls within my own circle, a circle closed on the outside; and, with all its elements alike, every sphere is opaque to the others which surround it . . . In brief, regarded as an existence which appears in a soul, the whole world for each is peculiar and private to that soul."

Against which, McDowell, "Singular Thought and the Extent of Inner Space," p. 249:
"In disconnecting experience from the external world, the fully Cartesian picture makes it problematic how the items it pictures can be anything but dark . . . it seems plausible that if we conceive propositional attitudes on the same principles, as occupants of the same autonomous inner realm, we make it no less problematic how it can be that they have a representational bearing on the world."

And cf. Jackson, *Michael Jackson in His Own Words*,
"We used to do these club shows, and this one lady—you probably know what she did—but I thought it was awful. I was around six, and she was one of those stripteasers, and she would take her drawers off, and a man would come up, and they would start doing—aw man, she was too funky. Ugh! That, to me, was awful!"

15: "This! is North and Clybourn! The next stop is Clark and Division. Doors open on the left! at Clark and Division."

18: Cf. Josh Frank, *Fool the World: An Oral History of the Pixies*: "Otto von Bismarck said 'If you want to fool the world, tell the truth.' He said it in 1889, when he fooled Prussia into war to create a little place to call home. (We now know it as Germany.) But a hundred years later in 1989, it was still not only true but about to be proven, or at least experimented with for the first time in a landscape of sound."

18: V. Pixies, "Gigantic"

19: After Berryman: "The poem, then, whatever its wide cast of characters, is essentially about an imaginary character (not the poet, not me) named _____, a white American in early middle age who has suffered an irreversible loss and talks about himself sometimes in the first person, sometimes in the third, sometimes even in the second."

19: Cf. Notley, "White Phosphorus"

20: [Marginal note in manuscript: "Further clarification needed here: just note it in passing."]

21: V. Kyd's *The Spanish Tragedy*.

21: Cf. Smith, "Kiss me kiss me kiss me/ Your tongue is like poison"

"Summer of Love"
The Post Cereal tradition began when C. W. Post made his first batch of "Postum," a cereal beverage, in a little white barn in Battle Creek, Michigan. With that step, he entered the brand new cereal retail industry and became a vital part of American breakfast history.

"J. Beer"
Cf. Gibson: "The sky above the port was the color of television tuned to a dead channel."

"The Paste Man"
Superglue was in veterinarian use for mending bone, hide, and

tortoise shell by at least the early 1970s. The inventor of cyanoacrylates, Harry Coover, said in 1966 that a superglue spray was used in the Vietnam War to retard bleeding in wounded soldiers until they could be brought to a hospital.

"Flowers":
Cf. Coleridge: "But where the ship's huge shadow lay/ The charming water burnt alway/ A still and awful red."

"Swift Boat Veteran for Beauty"
1. V. Teenager, "So Sad about You": "Jump start my heart with antifreeze."
2. V. Hamlet, 1.v: "As I perchance hereafter shall think meet/ To put an antic disposition on."

"Total Information Awareness"
V. Thomas Friedman, "Four Reasons to Invade Iraq." *Slate* 12 Jan. 2004. "The real reason for this war—which was never stated—was to burst what I would call the 'terrorism bubble,' which had built up during the 1990s. This bubble was a dangerous fantasy, believed by way too many people in the Middle East. This bubble said that it was OK to plow airplanes into the World Trade Center, commit suicide in Israeli pizza parlors, praise people who do these things as 'martyrs,' and donate money to them through religious charities. This bubble had to be burst, and the only way to do it was to go right into the heart of the Arab world and smash something—to let everyone know that we, too, are ready to fight and die to preserve our open society."

"Bob Hope Is Not a Plan"
The reader will observe that the question here is about essential truth, or about the truth that is essentially related to existence, and that is precisely for the sake of clarifying it as inwardness or as subjectivity that the knives are drawn.

Also, cf. Longfellow, *The Song of Hiawatha*:
And the smoke rose slowly, slowly,
Through the tranquil air of morning,
First a single line of darkness,
Then a denser, bluer vapor,
Then a snow-white cloud unfolding.

"Flowers"
Cf. Kafka, "Give It Up!"

"Trapped in the Closet"
This poem was stimulated by the account of the production of R. Kelly's R&B opera *Trapped in the Closet*: it was related that the singer/director found his own project inexplicable, "something that has never happened."

"Globe"
Cf. Penn Warren, "Love Recognized."

"Lives of the Poets"
Instead of these facile and revolting lines, please substitute:

Henry headed out to the tundra yesterday.
He left our model Pizza Hut behind

with parking lot lights that really light up
at twilight and the kids playing *Pac-Man*

while their mother cries in the restroom.
There's a reason money looks the way it does,

which I'd tell you if I had the inclination.
Then we got to the town where all the girls

wore faded T-shirts with words like "No"
or "Smile." My nose bled all that spring.

"Flowers"
Cf. Ritsos, "The Absent One"

"Speak Yon Undiscovered Towers"
Cf. Césaire: "des mots, ah oui, des mots! mais
des mots des sang frais, des mots qui sont
des raz-de-marée et des érésipèpes
des paludismes et des laves et des feux
de brousse, et des flambées de chair,
et des flambées de villes . . ."

"The Love Song of Lee Harvey Eliot"
V. Matthew 24:16. Also, Jühren Fohrmann, "From Literary
Utopia to the Utopia of Subjectivity," p. 293: "By projecting
utopia into the future, one could imagine a non-starting and a
non-ending process, which was nonetheless still guided by a
utopian impetus. The utopian impetus was itself now only
attainable by abolishing time. Kant called this condition 'the end
of all things.'"

"Theses on Failure"

Quotes from Marx's "Theses on Feuerbach," 1845, are presented in W. Lough's translation, Progress Publishers (USSR, 1969), available at:

marxists.org/archive/marx/works/1845/theses/theses.htm

"Sonnets to Morpheus"

62. Asked why he chose the code name Trinity for the first atomic test, Robert Oppenheimer replied, "Why I chose the name is not clear, but I know what thoughts were in my mind. There is a poem of John Donne, written just before his death, which I know and love. From it a quotation:

As west and east

In all flat maps—and I am one—are one,

So death doth touch the Resurrection."

63. Cf. Riding, "My eyes, my mouth, my hovering hands, my intrasmutable head: wherein my eyes, my mouth, my hands, my head, my body-self, are not such mortal simulacrum as everlong you builded against very-death, to keep you everlong in boasted death-course, neverlong?"

64. V. Carter Family, "Sad and Lonesome Day":

Oh, they carried my mother to the burial ground

Oh, they carried my mother to the burial ground

Oh, they carried my mother to the burial ground

I watched as the bearers let her down

65. Cf. "When Lilacs Last in the Dooryard Bloom'd":

I fled forth to the hiding receiving night that talks not,

Down to the shores of the water, the path by the swamp in the dimness,

To the solemn shadowy cedars and ghostly pines so still.

67. V. Genesis 10:9

69: Cf. Shakespeare, Sonnet 129

70: Cf. Lacan, *Écrits*, p. 208: "The subject's aggressiveness here has nothing to do with animals' aggressiveness when their desires are frustrated. This explanation, which most seem happy with, masks another that is less agreeable to each and every one of us: the aggressiveness of a slave who responds to being frustrated in his labor with a death wish." (trans. Fink)

71. The Heideggerian echoes here are deliberate.

"The Perfumed Crypt"

77. One of the great works of 1930s poetic realist cinema, *Le jour se lève* was Marcel Carné's fourth collaboration with screenwriter and poet Jacques Prévert. In this compelling story of obsessive sexuality and murder, the working-class François (Jean Gabin) resorts to killing in order to free the woman he loves from the controlling influence of another man.

79. V. Stevens, "A High-Toned Old Christian Woman"

81. "'Ostensive definition' may be defined as 'any process by which a person is taught to understand the use of words other than by the use of other words.' Suppose that, knowing no French, you are shipwrecked on the coast of Normandy: you make your way into a farmhouse, you see bread on the table, and being famished, you point at it with an inquiring gesture. If the farmer thereupon says 'pain,' you will conclude, at least provisionally, that this is the French for 'bread.'" Russell, *Human Knowledge: Its Scope and Limits*, p. 61.

82. Redford and Hoffman, although only alluded to and indeed not really 'characters,' are in a quite precise sense the most important personages in the poem, and perhaps in the book as a whole. Just as the angry little dog, observing the farmer's market, melts into Black Francis, and the latter is not wholly

distinct from Mary the color scientist, so all the words are one word, and all the events meet in their cinematic representation. What the actors enact, in fact, is the thing I can only gesture at. The whole passage from Ben Bradlee's memoir is of great ontological interest: Just after two in the morning on May 16, 1973, I got a call from Bernstein. He was calling from a public telephone nearby, to say that he and Woodward had to see me right away. In a scene from a le Carre spy novel, they sat down silently in my living room and handed me a memo, written a few hours earlier by Woodward after a dramatic encounter with Deep Throat. Specifically, Deep Throat had said, "Everyone's life is in danger." That concentrated my mind for real.

87: Benjamin: "As soon as Kafka was sure of his ultimate failure, everything else succeeded for him like a dream."

88. Cf. Ashbery, *Flow Chart*:

Then, when I did that anyway, I was not so much charmed as
    horrified
by the construction put upon it by even some quite close
    friends,
some of whom accused me of being the "leopard man" who
    had been terrorizing
the community by making howl-like sounds at night, out of
    earshot
of the dance floor.

89. Cf. Adorno: "This disappointment is none other than the disappointment of a child who reads Hauff's fairy tale and mourns because the dwarf, though no longer misshapen, did not get a chance to serve the duke his pâté Suzeraine."

"Mary, Color Scientist"

Cf. Frank Jackson, "Epiphenomenal Qualia": "Mary is a brilliant scientist who is, for whatever reason, forced to investigate the world from a black and white room *via* a black and white television monitor. She specializes in the neurophysiology of vision and acquires, let us suppose, all the physical information there is to obtain about what goes on when we see ripe tomatoes, or the sky, and use terms like 'red', 'blue', and so on. She discovers, for example, just which wavelength combinations from the sky stimulate the retina, and exactly how this produces *via* the central nervous system the contraction of the vocal chords and expulsion of air from the lungs that results in the uttering of the sentence 'The sky is blue'. (It can hardly be denied that it is in principle possible to obtain all this physical information from black and white television, otherwise the Open University would of *necessity* need to use color television.) What will happen when Mary is released from her black and white room or is given a color television monitor? Will she *learn* anything or not? It seems just obvious that she will learn something about the world and our visual experience of it. But then it is inescapable that her previous knowledge was incomplete."

ACKNOWLEDGMENTS

Another Chicago Magazine: "The Perfumed Crypt"

The Canary: "Sonnets to Morpheus" (2, 6, 8, 10)

Come Hither: "Flowers," "Flowers," "Flowers"

Denver Quarterly: "The Waste Land" (sec. 5), "No One Here Gets Out Alive"

Lo-Ball: "Theses on Failure"

Milk/Big Bridge: "Total Information Awareness," "Swift Boat Veteran for Beauty"

MiPoesias: "Bob Hope is Not a Plan," "Lives of the Poets"

MoonLit: "Trapped in the Closet," "Summer of Love," "Globe"

War and Peace: "Mary, Color Scientist"

Thanks to Canarium Books and its glorious editors: Josh, Lynn, Nick, and Robyn. Too many people contributed to the writing of this book to attempt to recognize them all. But I owe a deep debt of gratitude to Joel Craig, who saw most of these in their first versions, and Judith Goldman for essential guidance on the last stages. A tip of the hat to the Poetry Collection of University at Buffalo, the State University of New York, as well as Douglas Lavin and Harvard Library Special Collections, for help with the cover.

John Beer's poems and criticism have appeared in *Denver Quarterly*, *Verse*, *MAKE*, *Chicago Review*, *The Canary*, *Crowd*, *The Brooklyn Rail*, *War and Peace*, and elsewhere. He lives in Chicago, where he works as a theater critic for *Time Out Chicago*.